I0192711

Elegy for the 21st Century

Catherine McGuire

FUTURECYCLE PRESS

www.futurecycle.org

Library of Congress Control Number: 2016951192

Copyright © 2016 Catherine McGuire
All Rights Reserved

Published by FutureCycle Press
Lexington, Kentucky, USA

ISBN 978-1-942371-15-1

This is dedicated to all those trying to make their way in turbulent times, trying to keep their humanity in a machine-consumed culture.

Contents

— III —

Interlude

— IV —

Synchronicities

All the signs are pointing to it
the little arrows on the graph
the dead needles on the fir
the mute gesturing in the corner
Read your chart   observe the fortune
in the wrong house   retrograde
transiting duplicities square your sum

This is the Age of Acquiring
shifting magnetic cupidities drive the Wheel
secret springs of cash upwell   recede
taking us with them into dark caves, hardened silos
Market torsion has us screwed
Chinese finger-cuffed   the stocks
pin us publicly   the man behind the curtain
has fled   leaves us holding

Full moon has taken cloud protection
bulking around it   they block access
to our fave celeb   *Noli me tangere*
Signs and portents   covens of crows
wheel above   Pegasus has trampled the Crab
and Orion raped Cassiopeia last night
Call 911

Give us this day
our daily pesticidal soup
and forgive us our plastic surgeries
for we have become botoxed
against our flaws, forever Amen

Recombinant dreams task us: *Observe*
how your desires worm-hole the cosmos
calling forth demonic echoes
Nightmares, outed   wander headlines

looking for a story more suited
to their talents

In the streets, revenant mythologies
camouflaged as floodlit mural faces
paper smiles   six-pack hubris
infiltrate believers' carnivales
tie us to their kites as ballast   a song
stuck in mental grooves   replays
ad infinitum   —can't touch that—
Hera's got a cameo on *Guiding Light*

Quantum cosmonauts drill the minutiae
they believe in the god particle
but their strings have tangled
Synaptic sequences   re-engineered
for the best and the brightest
split the species   grow blue grain on salt marshes
send questing nanos lotioning into your veins
shooting deoxyribonucleic craps

The cultural autopsy lingers
in opposition to our stars
the gods pick through our landfills
holding up the trashed   the pickled
hosting the has-beens on game shows
Pan plays us all as pipes

We have split the infinitive   but it returns
to haunt us   The cosmic take-out window
is closing—what do you want?

The Apocalypse Goes Unnoticed in Newtown, CT

No one needs predictions there.
And on Turkish borders, huddled tents
have no preps for crisis. Trenton slums,
the barrios of Rio, the drained and droughty deltas
of Tigris, or Sudan—Apocalypse can knock
and enter; no one will care.
Which is to say, the world is always ending;
our treasures crumble, dust to dust.
The myth-inflated bogeys threaten
while, behind our backs, our futures rust.

Looking for Coins and Guns; Pray for Our Nation

—sign in a pawnshop window

In the bone-cold afternoon, December 26th,
the crack of a rifle splits
the damp silence, snaps like a twig:
crack! crack! crackcrackcrack—

Someone got a gun for Christmas.
Someone thinks he's Wyatt Earp.

Or a gangster, more like.
Crack! Blam! There is no flutter or thrash—
it's just what-the-hell shooting.
I hope he's aiming away.
I hope there's a house in between.
I hope there's a gun safe.

The neighbor got hauled away by cops
on Christmas Eve, when a drunken rave
about Apocalypse ended
with a waved gun.
I watched the spot-lit drama from a window:
him in the flashlights' glare, hands raised, pleading,
No gun, no gun!

But of course they found it.
Eventually, gave it back.

Foreclosure

And so I says to him, *Marvin,*
get a grip! It's only a house,
we'll live; we have each other.

But it hit him hard—the big TV
wasn't even paid off; the tile
he'd laid himself. I went back

on the sly; watched them trash it out—
honestly! All of it right into a dumpster!
I shouldn't have watched;

dear god—I had to stop on the shoulder
and vomit, on the way back
to Marv's sister's place. Never told him.

So *that* wasn't it. It was just everything,
I guess—pension gone; house gone;
Medicare fighting his claims—that

and the gun in their bedroom.
It was too handy, I guess.

Pit Stop

This is no tourist trailer parked beside us:
a cold dawn fingers
rusted ladder rungs curving
up to the dented roof, open-air "attic"
piled with summer clothes in garbage bags,
a coil of hose, buckets that might hold oats
or old shoes. Their featureless aluminum box
wheeled onto blacktop off the main road,
to the fringe of this roadside park
among the Bounders' and Outlanders'
expandable rooms and sleekly furled awnings,
hasn't moved since Wall Street hit a pothole
got a flat and swerved,
sending their lives off the edge
they'd spent years clinging to.

The bike tied to the back
is unhooked for the graveyard shift
at the Highway Gas'N Go.
She cooks silently at a charcoal grill—
The hot plate burnt out, she told me last week.
The white poly deck chairs and TV trays
create the dining room
that doesn't fit inside. They eat
with their backs to the rest of us—she's slim,
he's hefty, with long gray-streaked hair.
They don't socialize; don't use the concrete clubhouse
or showers or play bingo or cards.
Brown and green empties roll loose,
tinkle like wind chimes under the wheels
as cedars waggle admonitory fingers
over the rust-speckled, once mobile
home.

I hear them inside, though.
Morning is just another excuse to drink;
noon a rendezvous with Oprah;
evening a cold bike ride to the edge
of the interstate which is endlessly
leaving them behind.

The World According to Fine Print

I.

This product is not warranteed
*   against any failure, loss, non-functionality...*

It lives in negation—tiny barbs waiting
to claw back hope. Like vast atomic spaces,
it mostly means nothing—
and means it sincerely.

The user agrees to allow the manufacturer to create
*   files with proprietary information,*
*   profiles, beacons; to sell data...*

Threads, gossamer sticky
like webs, like old loves regretted.
Read them and weep.

II.

Words as shackle,
hidden slipknot noose.
Words that do not want to be read—
undead words; they will eat you,
given time.

On the fourth page of 5pt. type:
It has been explained to me
that this procedure could lead to disfigurement,
debilitation or death, and I accept this waiver...
Buried in kaleidoscopic prose,
activated by your signature:
I accept this waiver of responsibility...
*   I accept this waiver...*
*   I accept this...*

III.

The Age of Fine Print, when it is remembered,
may seem like a nightmare
that held the dreamers
paralyzed by the echo:
nyah, nyah, fingers crossed—now you're It.

Cleveland: Unlucky Number

One home in thirteen empty,
that thirteenth family set wandering,
the albatross mortgage dead around their necks.
To whom do they tell their tale?

This one is coffined—cheap plywood
closing windows like dead eyes.
Next door is newly orphaned, ghosted
by the family who fled last night or last week—
the windows unclouded, the lawn still green.

Two doors up, a third—rivulets of black rain
graffiti the trim, as does paint sprayed in gang-spoor,
red and black, on the door.
A block away, one like roadkill, vulture-ridden:
insides gutted of appliances and lamps,
even the copper veins are stripped;
hacked corpse left rotting.

Across town, duplex row house doubly forsaken,
red bricks sprayed with hot orange note—
Do Not Enter—UNSAFE. Curling up a hill,
three half-baked shells;
the bubble burst before their studs were dry;
the cul-de-sac now twice a dead end.

Nearby, a foreclosure sign: the bank is looking
for some brass-knuckle investor to drop-kick the old widow
still living inside. She peers from between dishtowel curtains
at the clear-windowed box with its colorful descriptions
of her family's much-loved rooms.

The blight proceeds unevenly: an unseen loft
above a vacant grocery;
a pretty yellow bungalow, front porch strewn
with collapsed lawn chairs, trike, plastic buckets, bags of trash.
Some blocks have just two families left;
some are whole—for now.

Take a walk; count thirteen as you go; picture it.

Eating at the Poorhouse

Chipped red brick behemoth squatting
on a hill above the freeway.

Would you like to start with a drink?
I recommend the chardonnay...

Rolling fields, cover-cropped with malls,
U-Store-Its   black-topped lots

  an appetizer? The stuffed portabellas are wonderful.

Nineteenth-century project   help the poor maintain
self-respect   with hard work.

Our special tonight is pork tenderloin
grilled with asparagus and caramelized onions.

Broad porch   bleached bentwood rockers
workhouse reclaimed   renovated   transformed.

With chicken, you have a choice of garlic mashed potatoes
or saffron pilaf...

Inmate dorm rooms   now rented
a hundred a night   to lovers   families
here for tennis courts   spa   rose gardens.

julienne of green beans...

Caramel oak floors   creak
soft groans   old voices soaked in.
How many died?

and green salad with raspberry vinaigrette.

Overseer's notebook page   poster-sized on the wall.
The Herculean scrawl: "146 men, 89 women,
48 not able to work   due to disability."

Fresh pepper or a bit of parmesan?

Other walls muralled   rich colors obscuring
pragmatic Victorian plaster   and molding.

Is that cooked to your liking?

Deep booths   stained like old oak   ceiling lamps'
squat glass mushroom authenticity   weighty amber pints
recall dinners of the inner circle.

Our Ruby Stout goes well with that steak.

Cigars and port   while inmates cleared   swept   washed,
working off their bread and small beer.

We have a scrumptious dessert tray—cheesecake
tiramisu, mousse...

Young staff   cropped hair   tattoos,
gel pens tucked behind an ear,
unhaunted   by ancestral servitude.

Shadows

The old men cast their shadows on the street.
In faded parkas, dazed by sun or gin,
they wear cast-off Nikes, large upon their feet.

Who knows if they are fakes or genuine?
The homeless, nameless men who line the curbs,
they hold their signs like tattered mannequins.

Their numbers swell, their desperate pleas reverb—
A dollar for a bite of food,
Will work, God bless—it reaches to disturb

our concentration; deftly spoil our mood:
Dare we give, or will our gift be spent
for a pint of Henry's or home-brewed?

Is it tough love or abandonment
to leave them tasting only their defeat?
How will we answer to the indigent?

And so we grapple: Greed and/or deceit?
The old men cast *our* shadows on the street.

Grand Street North

I.

Beyond the plowed zone, where signs
shout resurrection, Grand Street turns into treeless
stucco blocks, homes of asphalt clapboard,
metal doors; walls tattooed with gang spoor. Nothing
trickles down here but rain. Billboard
starlets sell hope, their paper smiles hugely
empty. Along the exits, old cars pile like rusted bones:
a Fairlane with cinderblock wheels and no voice,
an eyeless Bug with flattened roof.

It is not apathy—paralysis comes in cans
and bottles; the cloned yearnings that leach
character leave a flavorless day.
The fragile things have fled—glass, children,
dreams. Windows are cardboard, metal, wood;
no vision, no exit. Scabrous iron-mesh gate—
rusting spider's web with no prey. Victims gone,
the hunters hunt each other. Tight faces,
whispered plans, broken needles in the gutter.

Conspiracy of generations laid bare, unseen;
a city diminished by pain unacknowledged.
The cripple feigns health; the leprosy proceeds.

II.

Evening slides in on the backs of thunderheads.
Sunset fingers a doorway split by anger, bruised
and sagging. A pile of clothes wakes, rises,
called by neon hieroglyphs and the smell of bread.

Sifting through garbage, the wind finds nothing;
the dogs take all. News serves to stuff cracks;

what serves to heal? Like moths,
survivors hurl themselves at night,
seeking ecstasy in glowing moments,
cupping extruded joy to their lips.

Effervescent amber seduces the tongue,
gently steals the future, rolling her trick
into the nearest doorway. Burning tires
fill the air with toxins of rage. Ill-marked
detours are ignored by leaden travelers
who left the freeway hours—no, years—
ago. Which ramp toward escape?

The spill that stains this place is moving,
sending poison rivulets into finer neighborhoods.
Containment is impossible; some want
to bomb it into parking lots,
flattening roaches and flowers. Pave it over.

III.

A shoebox house: blowsy hydrangeas
fading on a balding lawn, blankets
on dusty windows, a coat of blue paint
against despair. Broken bottles
like empty mouths press into the fence.

Along the frayed windowsills, dead leaves
trace their memoirs. This house, this block
is *Available* from a distant keeper,
selling like thrift store junk for a pittance.
Upper windows leak dirty rain like runny mascara.
A stick-figure tenant with a dried-apple face,
khaki pants, a stained shirt, watches the afternoon
blister the tavern sign across the road.

A black cat studies dead flies on the sidewalk
as an ivory chemise tumbles the block, hugs
a hydrant. The corner lot is a brick pile,
construction halted until a reason can be found.

An old woman in a dirt-colored coat stops
at the tavern for a lottery ticket. In her mind
she is young, smooth as a cigarette ad.

Kubla Can't

If Kubla Khan did currently
his stately pleasure dome decree,
he'd first need to get permission
from the planning board commission;
and only if his building specs
had all been duly scanned and checked,
and sent out for neighborhood review,
to the City Clerk of Xanadu.
Still—he'd run afoul of codes
that set the arches' max stress loads;
the caves of ice would have to go—
not ecological, you know.
And as for "deep romantic chasm,"
unless it's wetlands, *no one* has 'em!
He'd be lucky to build at all
near anything alluvial;
what with riparian setbacks,
he'd never get his cul-de-sac
near *any* "sacred river." Ha!
Much less a sex basilica!
He wants a pleasure dome? Good lord!
protest the neighbors and school boards,
There's zoning laws for porno sites!
Fat chance he'd ever get the right
to build on ground where children gather;
a "lofty" plan would fare no better—
he'd find out there's no "laissez-faire"
if he tried to build the dome in air!
He's drunk on the milk of Paradise,
but our zoning board will set him right.

Suburb on the Edge of Nowhere

Tract homes corralled by cinder block walls,
blank-eyed, gelded, tame,
huddle like frightened sheep
in a wilderness of wheat.

Hours from any mall, the four short streets curve
as if to impede invasive traffic.
The lone tractor circling pays them no heed.
Their perfect gutters slowly fill with chaff.
In the stillness, no burger wrappers tumble.
Midnight falls with the weight of silence, unbroken
by car alarms, blared radios, late streetball.

Whatever delirium began a 'burb in Wheat Town
has passed; it stands alone
one long dusty block from the feed store,
the post office single-wide, and City Hall's
refurbished train station, the summer night sky
shining down, unseen.

Saturday: Anytown

The kid, sixteen, has a smoker's cough;
he hacks and leans into the engine well.
The air is oily, tangled with gas
and the percussion of metal interrogation.

Nearby, the river rushes over basalt; birds
try out their courting songs.
They fight with mowers and hot rods. And lose.
Unseen, a neighbor fires up a chainsaw.
Another starts a blower, turning gasoline
into air to push leaves, dirt, twigs
across a lawn; to push hearing into deafness.

A spiral of gray rising across the street
from the leaf-and-cardboard trash fire
sends Vesuvian scraps spiraling
lazy to the lawn. These weekend rituals
punctuate the workday shuttle—workers
like bees returning to their hives.

But bees can no longer smell
the opening flowers; diesel
and exhaust now bind their subtle pheromones,
killing the scent, losing the call.
Trapped in a man-made fog,
they miss their aim, sometimes by inches.
Stamens fold untouched, and the bees starve.

Men wander the grass as sun warms the lawns
they've squared and neutered with their sprays.

Construction

Another All Drug rises on scraped earth.
Drivers, halted at the new stoplight,
glance over at thin brick veneer
layered on steel beams and waferboard.
Highway 20 has new curbs: concrete
berms like welts,
like ritual scarification,
outline the future parking lot.

In a backhoe cab, a recent high school grad
gently steers the rusty steel claw
to dip into a truck bed,
scoop out red clay scavenged
from some other dig. He plops it
in the narrow channel allotted
for trees and plants—first rain will
turn that cheap dirt into concrete, too,
but a steel bore will puncture it
enough to ram a sapling in,
and if the entombed roots are crushed,
that's someone else's job.
His union wage pays gas
and a bit for food. The clerks who clock in
under the fluorescent lights won't
get any more than the Walmart clerks
across the way. They'll live uninsured, on food stamps—
crushed like sapling roots.

Living On Food Stamps and the $150 They Get From Nielsen

A prolapsed couch, some blankets,
a punched-down pillow make a nest
to watch TV from; the tinker-toy tower of gadgets
is piled black and silver in one crowded corner—
topped by the Nielsen box. Here are your prime
viewers: unemployed, living on food stamps
and an equal mite from their willing exposure
to Nielsen's counters. The furniture's hocked
except for that big-screen altar they sacrifice
their lives to. After a year, unemployment
ran out—the queues for jobs still impossibly long.
The day is full of bacon sandwiches,
Cup-a-Soup, and prayer. They light
their HD "candle," let the glow flood the room,
flood their hours with Judge Judy,
with their peephole into rooms of other lives
more fraught than theirs—praying, rapt,
for rich teens marooned on islands
who are surviving on their wits.

Squatter's Flag

The time dwindles, the year dissolves—
rain stirs the ivy leaves
as Portland's steady drizzle spoils
its eighteenth day. The hills
hold snow like heavy cream, but here
frozen mud and dead leaves
are worn away, cell by cell,
their passage imperceptible,
like seconds in a fading year.

The highway spins off-ramps like fraying cord
lashed to the grid of streets.
Under bridges, citizen phantoms
weave fragments and slag into fragile cocoons.
Extruded cinder blocks anchor beds,
bags; possessions that the winds covet.
Sulfurous street lamps pierce the shadows,
waxing robust on hollow cheeks.
No one stands straight here.

As headlights strafe black plastic walls,
they burst upon the Flag: vivid
red/white bars cross girders, a square of deep starry night,
a staunch barrier to cold, rain,
and godless communism. By morning
it is gone—someone objects
to free PR for Liberty,
someone rejects bright colors
in a graveyard. Or something.

For the Forgotten

With half-lives far shorter
and story lines tainted
with poisons anathematic
to US hope and gumption,
the towns swept by earthquake
flood or fire continue
long past our fickle
spot of attention.
Small bodies like seaweed
washed up on the beaches.
Like comets, they drew us
the film clips, news columns
of breathless outpouring:
foodstuffs, used clothing
bandages, water—
once "safely" in refugee
camps, they're forgotten.
When did you last think of Haiti,
New Orleans or Chile?
How long past disaster
does your focus linger?

— II —

All Models Are Wrong, But Some Models Are Useful

whether or not you believe in
the Black Swan
whether or not your nights are troubled
by special envoys, giant muons
and chicken-shit theories
of fibonacci flu
whether or not you have met
the cashier of your hopes
who is ready to check you out
though you keep reading fantastic binary meanings
into the newsstand rags' titles
whether or not
your debt card says UnAligned
when you swipe it
and your FreeCell game shuffles crooked
and throws a Jack from the bottom
for a loyal flush
and even if you mount a fervent campaign
to advocate
deterministic chaos
in all your affairs—
there is a special place reserved
in N-space
for those who believe intelligence
is contrived for the ensemble
and solitaries constitute
their own prime numbers

Japan Washes Ashore in Oregon

I.

Two years later, debris scuttles onto the shingle:
fishing boats, brass bowl, a temple gate,
scrap wood, a window frame, shop sign—
there's no closure to some wounds.

Buried in black and beige sand drifts:
someone's smashed mirror, holding
fractured clouds, broken sky.

II.

Unseen, uninvited, radiation floats
then burrows. The vast currents
that trawl the sea
leave long, invisible streamers.
The truth leaks more slowly
than cesium, plutonium, tritium.
Data, well buried. Don't connect
neighbor's cancer,
the slowly dying trees, those shriveled,
Cerberus-headed sunflowers.
Don't think about hungry ghosts
devouring flesh and leaf
in the night.

Salmonelle

From the streams where they spawned;
from wide rivers where, they say,
you could walk across on them—gone

like ink fading on a page;
photos, graying, know the tale.
From wide rivers gone, they say.

Yaquina, Rogue, Deschutes, Nehal-
em: liquid silver journeys fade.
Photos, graying, show the tale

but, salmon-mute, they can't persuade
us to act decisively before
those liquid silver journeys fade

for good. And still we ignore
the fade of silver that should have caused
us to act decisively, before?

We'll tell our children of that awesome
parade of silver; fishy causeway
up the streams where they spawned.

You could walk across on them. Gone.

Symbiosis

Planted by Columbia Slough—née swamp—
near brackish ponds and bronze tangled weeds,
the rippled-tin sheds, the squat concrete barns and mills
collect their own bracken: cast-off goods adrift and sinking.

Corrugated metal walls, moss-pocked concrete
and slurry heaps of black tar vie with brambles
for the parking lots. Rusting motors accrete
iron-eating barnacles: fern, moss and lichen,

surrealistic sculptures wrought
of nature's rape. The entropy of decay
has taken hold of plant and machine both;
dying slow together, they create

a metamorphic soup—evolution's flotsam
in a weed and concrete sea.

For the 21st Century: Elegy on Six Monitors

Grainy pixels coalesce and flow.
En-framed: ten feet of hall, immortalized
in Dada brilliance, endless, empty—now
saved to disk. Another screen espies
grayscale daisies, chessboard of weeds;
squad of eight-horsepower pawns in check,
rusting door locks, relict of keys.
A third scans sky like an oily wreck:
slimy clouds roil and snake a sun
catacombed perpetually behind steel ranks—
towers fractaled; cracks that blossom
at the wind's insistence. A fourth is blank.
A fifth is fuzz. The last screen's frozen and
shows lobes of smoke, door handle, one hand.

2040: Salvage Party

To all back at Holly Street:
I hope this finds you well.
I hope you have a loaf to spare
for the one who carries this to you.

The coast is desolate—swept clear
of buildings, all scrap salvaged
or overgrown. The rumors of
an alien settlement are false—

at least, we've seen no one. Fish
aren't plentiful, but suffice—
we should be back by fall with salmon
dried and salted. We avoid the deformed.

Rain is constant; the chill is biting—
wish I could bring that back to you for relief.
Mark is gathering seedlings; his naïve hope
to coddle them back East is touching.

Enough—paper and ink run out. My love
goes with this messenger and hope
that we will celebrate the Harvest
that I will be there to gather.

A United State of Amnesia

Rolling fog of days,
dropped stitches;
history unravels
behind us. Quavering
illusion—solid ground?
Hands twitch; thumb thrusts;
mouse swirls,
hardwired.
Withering synapse—
factoid fog.

Sunlit morning—
scarlet poppies gleam.
Steaming coffee, breeze,
soft peace vanishing
unrecorded—no soundtrack,
that modern memory aid.
Only adrenalin: relentless
pounding lays traces
in neural folds.

Atrophied by gadgets,
senses dim,
white-noised into oblivion.
Tweets unsourced,
repeated—tsunami
of trivia floods out
structure, meaning—
battered wreckage
slimed with lies.

Oh, History!
The second casualty
after Truth.

Invasives

In the fields, grain is prostrate,
dying slow and blonde;
the culverts are snowed with chaff.
Framing each ten-acre square,
shadows tangle in dark brambles
that twine like fairy tale
around a collapsed cottage
that is not gingerbread.

This county has no use for myth;
their super-shined Chevys are symbol enough
for what they want to say;
the gentle undulations of corrugated steel
sketch the extent of their ambivalence.
Living, as they do, with the certainty of decay,
farm women scoff at Botox ads,
look ruefully in non-magic mirrors,
content themselves with boxed perms.
The men pound another hole in their belts, cushion
the vinyl tractor seats with carpet foam,
feel red dust settle on their sweat-soaked arms and faces—
a second skin for the day.

Here, the secret brotherhood of diazinon sprayers
walk the fields, backpacking plastic tubs with long hoses,
gently poisoning the dirt, removing bugs and weeds.
The damp breeze on their faces will gently poison them
but, without insurance, it will be no one's problem.
Materials Handling forms snow dining tables,
are shoveled discretely into the trash
that is discretely shoveled into thickets or swamps
far from the need to explain.

Harvest is one long vigil:
praying off rain clouds,
watching hay dry to tinder, weighing breeze,
tensing for stray sparks that could eat the season
in a single hot, smoky meal.
The leaves die back from fat
Cinderella-less pumpkins.
Hopes are threshed in this lean summer
against thin columns accounting
for too little,
where browning vines or nibbled fruit
predict anemic savings, perennial debt.

Here, the days shape up their dented version
of urban posh. In the town, FAST CASH
rolls out the dust-greasy pawned tools—
chop saws, hand trucks, rakes.
Daily, the flags of the nations—
Britain, US, France, Confederate—
appear across the old Ford lot
fluttering brash colors on the line
waving blankly at tourists
who flee down Highway 20.
Daily, the dancing, grin-pasted teen
with the pizza sign,
the line idling at Dutch Brothers,
the Denny's crowd.
Empty shops like dried seed pods gape
dusty and hollow.

Here, after-school groups have no official sanction
aside from warrior sports that "shape the man."
Basement ballet studios give recitals at the county fair
in costumes borrowed from the next town over.
The strawberry princess in her homemade gown
gets no free shopping sprees.

Nightly, teens circle their jalopies on vacant lots,
sit on hoods and tailgates, compare tattoos
under halogen glare.
There are plenty of drugs, but beer is the cheapest magic
for draping the lean evenings with glimmer and fizz.

Roads to the city, tough as tendrils,
tug away the enthusiasm,
leave the grain fields flat, dusty and still.

Reveille (or Taps)

Never have so many been warned so often about so much...

Without fail-proof memory or data,
I don't know if these apples are budding early;
don't know if fewer robins murder worms or fewer moles crater
my lawn. I see tomato vines curling
with some wilt or other. My fault?
Or climate? The train wreck's so slow
I barely see it; can't sense the gestalt;
the dawn spreads in the east, wet or dry. What do I know?
I'm just one of six billion (and that's just people)
who share this problem, and which part's mine?
A decade of global meetings, yet decline is steeper?
If they can't agree, who'll listen to me?
If only greed caused cancer, something *seen*,
or willful ignorance had a vaccine.

Drought in the Garden

As dry as feathers folded down
around the stems, parched leaves wither
in the heat. It is still;
everything waits for death or forgiveness
to cover the land. Even insects
are defeated by the harsh
judgment that glares one-eyed at those
who transgressed the subtle balance,
the interplanted wisdom of
the first days. What wisdom is left
is doled out sparingly to save
what is judged essential. Still
no sign, save the ever-widening
cracks in dry wood, no sign
that salvation is at hand
or anywhere else for that matter.
The thirsty ones have left already,
seeking other lands. Those
with roots into the marrow wait
unmoving, listen for the first
hiss of life flowing from
secret ponds.

Fracked (We Are)

The vast, deep pools of oil
(just when we'd gotten a taste for the stuff)
are rasping like the last suck from dry soil.

Someone figured out how to crack
shale, force toxic slush into weak seams
to blast apart, to fracture

rock, to bleed "condensates" in scummy spurts
that need cooking, screening—alchemy for which
we pay till it hurts.

Tearing apart miles of earth each day,
new ruptures spreading like tremors. Measurable
but perfectly safe, they say.

Isn't this like a junkie on his last relapse
who shoots heroin between his toes
because his arm veins have collapsed?

False Equivalence

These rolling grassy domes east of the highway—
some bald, some tonsured,
rising gently from flat, hay-bricked fields
with rumpled furrows.

I recite their names as I drive by—Buck Mountain,
Round Mountain, Hell's Hill—
I could look at them all day.
They do not appear in Oregon's asset column.
When they are listed at all,
they are *gravel, sand, Doug fir.*
They are platted for mud stucco houses
built with the gutted hill's wood and stone.
Those sinuous curves illuminating
the landscape are sacrificed
when you move in, fill your garages
with lime green Troy mowers
and bulbous-wheeled, scarlet ATVs
you will screech up/down the remaining hills,
gouging lopsided crop circles
and screaming with joy.

There is no way back.

It's been a subtle transformation,
a quickening morph
from sacred to raced;
shelter to shovelful.

The deepening shadows stroke the hills,
running indigo fingers through the blonde grass.
The stillness is manna—you can eat
but not hoard.
It feeds a deep need.

You say,
everyone desires equally.
I have my turquoise Chevy with chromed fins.

I say,
when your Chevy
is a thin layer of rust and blue,
let these hills still be caressed by these shadows
softly wearing off
the day's veneer.

Pacific Northwest 2012

Swifts thread the cedars towering
calm against unclouded blue, a chilly July
in a wet summer overpowering
heat-seeking plants. We know why
the climate's disarrayed, and yet
we're paralyzed, seduced by summer,
or deafened by the onslaught of betting
on two degrees, or six—Apocalypse Come, or
data hyped? Birds still chatter,
though some are missing; our gardens ripen
more or less. Can drought or famine matter
until they're at our doorstep, frightening
and much too late to stop?

Some season soon, we'll reap denial's crop.

Six-Course Apocalypse

The trailer in *Revelation,* as all trailers do,
pulled out the hot bits, the thrills—
we were fooled into thinking
it would be one Big Bang finale.

But no. You'd think we'd realize
how drama works.
This is a relentless episodic series
drawn out over a lifetime or two;
this is a full-course dinner
of crow and old hat.

The four Ninja Horsemen sneak
through the dark with masks and blackened tools,
dismount, and do more damage on foot.

Famine swathes the usual villages
and towns but covers its tracks
with news blurbs of CARE packages dropped
like manna. It goes upscale as anorexia
becomes the ultimate fashion goal;
it dopplegängs as empty calories
slowly infiltrating potbellied kids
who play World of Warcraft
until only their thumbs have muscles.

War calls itself Unrest and harvests
scores in villages, thousands in town,
then bolts before it can be Formally Declared.

Death, of course, is hard to disguise—
but data is an awesome camouflage: statistics,
like swarms of flies on carrion, fog the air,
smudge the actual count, the real cull.

And Disease? Well—hold on to your N95 masks,
my little chicks and piggies...

Spring Tide, Balboa

Rumors filled the week: full moon
and high tide *both*—Balboa
might go under. A party de rigueur.

Night found us at the cantina,
exploring an "Adios Mutha"—blue Curaçao
and six other liqueurs in a snifter.

The beach heat gave way to bodies pressed tight.
Arcade full of Skee-Ball, tang of Coppertone,
of citronella candles, of beer.

Rock and jazz from six different bars
wafted through the narrow, twinkle-lighted street.

We watched as the curb bordering the beach
was runneled, then overrun—
beach fires doused by the ocean's invasion,
a brownish-green tide swirled over fancy sandals.

We laughed as if we'd plotted the whole thing:
bars with sandbagged doors, the party sloshing
up and down the street. Seventies. Rare tidal surge.

Unrecognized taste of the future.

Can You Outrun a Tsunami?

...Race the Wave this weekend on the Oregon Coast.
—The Oregonian, *September 11, 2015*

Up the coastal highway, on poles and storefronts,
the poster's question blared: *Can you outrun...?*
Imagine the 12-foot wave, the wall
that slams like a fist towards you.
Imagine the roads toward the hills.
The 5K and 10K run scheduled for Saturday
will test your mettle. Let's have T-shirts
and hot dogs and TV coverage.
Ol' USA know-how will beat that monster—
hold a race up the hill, Lycra and headbands,
lithe limbs and Nikes pounding the asphalt
as the crowds cheer. Let the day be sunny.
Let no sign of high waves
disturb our fun.

Non-Zen-sical

I'm praying for the Zen view.
I'm desperately sick of
mad hatters and
revolutionary tea parties
and days churned with rational
blindness like planning
McDonald's bomb shelters.
I haven't time to sit
until my mind warps around
Creation and finds serenity
quivering in its cell.
I need a Porta-Zen,
a path that zips like people-movers
rushing travelers to their
delayed planes.
I need a cosmic super-glue
to jam those fragments of meaning
back into something my great-aunt
would be proud to display.
I believe we should do with less.
(That's what we'll be getting, anyway.)
I believe we should learn to
slow down—but that class meets
on my busy Tuesday.
So I'm praying for Zen—
a flash of enlightenment
before the final flash.

— III —

Dear Applicant

(fill your name in here)

Thank you for your resume,
which we received last month or so—
along with many thousands
sailing in from lay-off land.
We reviewed it thoroughly
for at least 15 seconds
before throwing it in the bin.
(You will be happy, we recycle.)

Sadly, you do not fit our needs;
you don't fit at all...did you think
you would?
You don't fit the profile
created by InstaSlave from
recycled statistics
about loyal employees and slackers—
not the right personality
for our Procrustean position.
Your handwriting shows you're too self-assertive,
according to our graphologist ($50,000 annual gross);
not right for our winning team
of tongue-lolling lapdogs—
there's a risk of too much self respect.

But we do thank you for your interest,
for your desperation—
it keeps us going
(it really does). If we ever have
another opening, be assured:
you will have to apply
all over again.

Sincerely,
The Management

A Long Day

Hunched over the screen,
tapping the keyboard—a long day
almost over. Soon he'll be
having pizza with the kids,
hearing wifely tidbits
from the neighborhood.
Cruising past the Vegas strip
and into the grid of homes.
Soon. A few minutes more.
It's always something last-minute
to nail him to the desk—
this one came up fast. He blinks,
sees the odd bit on the screen,
too big for a rock—it moves;
his fingers race frantically—
the white puff like a truck's backfire,
Predator rocket too fast to see.
Slam! into the target; now nothing
left on that Bagdad road but grit.
Quick surveillance—nothing.
Just the arm of someone
lying across the road. *Leave it
for the next shift.* He stands,
flips the "off duty" switch,
slips into a light jacket,
pushes in his chair,
heads through the glass door
into the heat of the late afternoon.

Demeter Moment

In a blank white cube of a room
at a plastic table
facing each other
halfway through your tale
of vague, tangled happenstance
weary plodding
resistant strangers' crisp indifference
ending here
a locked ward
sheltering your girl
whose life, already tragic
has turned down another dark path
hoping we can decipher
turn aside
the corruption somewhere
in her brain—
we look deeply into each other's eyes
sensing hope and hopelessness
linked by Demeter's aching cry
for her vanished child.

But Otherwise—Okay?

The language threading through the bill,
in pages layered like bitumen seams,
reams of dense wordage—the "war
on coal"—seeks to stop beheading mountains.

Strip-mine mutation: 500 mountains destroyed;
forests burned or trashed; blasting 600 feet down
because tunneling needs miners.
Mechanized draglines don't strike for overtime,
don't blow whistles.

Threatening to local villages, it says.

This wastage—once a tangled thicket,
   once sapling
      and bramble
        and moss—
dumped on graveled streams,
burying eddies of minnow and trout,
spring tadpoles inhumed.

Deer paths obliterated; warblers vanishing
as oak, hickory, spruce disappear. In deep graves under red soil:
ginseng, orchid,
   magnolia, sumac,
     holly, persimmon,
        salamander, crayfish, mussel.

Two thousand miles of streams buried.
Valleys drowned in sludge dams of "spoil."
Flattened acreage—the stumps of mountains—
sprayed with grass seed, abandoned,
out of sight.

Harmful to humans, the unearthed poisons,
harmful to children, dusty dregs—
higher rates of heart and lung disease, premature death.

Legislation pleading the only words that might sway
a human heart.

Conduit

*223-mile natural gas pipeline proposed through
southern Oregon*

A snake wriggling into the garden
across a neglected pen-and-paper boundary,
penetrating high desert scrub.
No—more like a poison spreading slow,
its snaky paths seeping across farms, forest.
Not quite. A mole tunneling, destroying roots. *Closer.*
A siege trench. *Closer.* A last desperate destructive spasm
to suck the dregs with a state-long straw,
ripping up, making wasteland, and as the pipe is laid
in the ditched devastation, a tremor at the source,
a hands-in-empty-pockets moment
making the whole damn thing moot.
Yeah.

Century Farm

Designation for family-owned more than 100 years

The river fog dampens his shirt
as he walks out—four a.m. The front cedars
are solid; the rest is mist—an acre of woods obscured.
As the red barn looms, that whiskery corrugation
of old cedar planks, he glances again
at that rotten corner brace. *Fix it—right after haying.*
But he's been saying that for years. Cows
begin their deep, thrumming moan.
Never fails to stir him, that sound, like keening
in some ritual bovine grief. He knows they just want grain.

The barn's dusty cave is like switching off the fog.
The pungent alfalfa-and-cow-piss tang as rich, in its way,
as the incense at Mass—though he'd never say that.
But it heralds his life's rituals as much as brass censers do.

His first memory: three years old, sitting in a wet cowpat, crying.
Monster face with flaring nostrils scared him backwards.
Dad laughing, bent double. Hay-breath cow sniffs him gently.
When he touches the velvet soft muzzle, he is soothed.

The cliff-dive of beef prices brings him back—each year
he comes closer to losing this place. News of billions
dropped in pin-striped laps brings a gut-wrenching rage.
Bastards. *Just drop it,* his wife keeps telling him. *What can you do?*
But them in their annual new limos don't know shit:
how land becomes part of you, like an arm or leg.
His great-granddad's headstone in the northwest corner,
neatly fenced.

His new neighbors plowed up the marigolds,
planted rhodies down their front path. Pretty.
But the prairie sun will crucify them this summer.
City dudes wanting store-display yards
instead of working with the earth. They'll learn.

Whistle Stop

The wind blows cool through the gorge,
shivering the roadside ferns, as the bus stops
at the town's only gas station. He steps off.
Sunset settles between far hills
like a glorious citron layer cake—
but he is focused on meeting his connections,
fuming at the absurdity of briefing reporters on the sly,
at the perverse containment of truth behind corporate facades,
the sudden doubling of security—
he's no Deep Throat; not even sure of the relevance
of his facts. But this isn't just another scandal;
those chickweed-framed bunkers, set like barrows
in scrubby fields, off-limits even to deer,
could make 9/11 look tame.
He spots the corner café rendezvous,
catches his breath; jay walks across Main
cursing the inscrutable paths of Fate, the pedantic tunnel vision
of employers, the urge of all reporters to create news
that rocks the world...and, yes, at himself
for abandoning the simplicity of blind duty.

Ticking Over the New Year

The streets are dry—a Christmas blessing.
Social outreach can get messy in winter—
checking on discharged residents, shooing bums
in from the cold. Steinway Terrace (an alley
in Astoria, Queens) is full of glittering trash—
a dry flocked Christmas tree sheds its dandruff,
powdering large cardboard crates angled suspiciously like shelter.
The paper cave holds Roger and Dale (his spaniel),
a milk crate on which rests his tattered book of Rimbaud,
a mug from NYU—class of '91, he says—
a logo pen and blank deposit slips,
a gift from US Bank. The slips hold poems scrawled
in angular, shaky script. "No competition for Arthur,"
he laughs. Not that Rimbaud cares. Nor others. Roger agrees
that it would be good to come to St. V's and get
his next batch of Zyprexa, maybe some dog food, a scarf, a meal.
But "someone will take all this—and then what?
Besides, I like the music," he laughs
as Tom Waits echoes off the bricks—he sings along—
"My piano's been drinking, not meeee."
He fumbles under his disintegrating parka and pulls out a beer,
pops the cap with his teeth, and offers me the first sip.
"To prosperity in the new year!" he laughs. "To peace on earth!
To equality and love for everyone!"
To Roger and the others, I think, sipping and handing it back.
From my overcoat pocket, I pull a Subway sandwich, bag of Oreos
and some black licorice; his face lights up.
"Merry fucking Christmas," he breathes.
With a handshake, we part.
Back at the curb, a parting gift from NYPD—
a parking ticket under the wiper of my VW bus.

Gary

"It's gotten hard," he said, shaking out a Lucky
from the pack, lighting, sucking nicotine.
"Bank slammed us with overdrafts, landlord
wants us out. Two jobs folded—
there's nothing in this county. Nothing."

Drizzle feathers his worn shearling coat.
He glances at me, away.
Under the anger, terror. At thirty,
strong, skilled, he chases two-bit jobs like mine.
Between rabbits, he tells me of the farms shut down
or selling out, of the rattle-trap car too complex
for him to fix. The job forms, the ad in Craigslist,
the silence. He dispatches the second rabbit,
cuts short its squeal with practiced aim.

He shrugs. "Might have to leave. Alaska,
shale fields. But moving costs money—what if
there's nothing there?"
I give him five bucks, offer him a rabbit,
let him have his pick of jams.
No handouts for single men.
Let them work, the Learjet crowd sneers.
Or let them starve.

Study

It's always the overnight shift.
He walks through each room,
checks the bed, bathroom, the wires
coiled on a cart, color-coded,
waiting to be glued to each patient.

They arrive with their pillows, wary—
each struggling with sleep.
He welcomes; starts the patter,
explains the night's routine.

*Once you fill out these forms, change to PJs
and watch TV. I'll be back to hook you up,
then we'll get you settled. Here's the breakfast menu.*
He glides from room to room, chunking tasks
in the usual order. Greet, settle, glue.

The myriad wires must connect perfectly,
so he gently abrades skin with a Q-tip,
explains why. Then body wires, the easiest,
before he measures the head for placement, uses ether-
based glue in hair, on scalp.
Used to be fishhooks, he comments.

The questions are curious, or panicky, or defensive—
he's heard it all. Five years as a tech,
watching through the camera as people toss, turn, snore—
plug 'em in, pluck 'em off—four or five per night.

With one eye on the monitors, he thinks back
to the mill job—different, yet not. Logs
rolled through, not people, but this, too, was routine,
with small variations. Twenty-two years. Plant closed;
he ended up here.

The Wiretappers' Ball

Viral ears have brambled, threaded
through the pillow talk of lonely joes,
boring into newshounds' calls, *kaptured* keystrokes.
Our shattered vision, cracked, susceptible
to ooze, to screws, to crews perusing.
Pierced by sly interrogatives,
official scrolls and documents are epitaphs
infected with Rumor-culosis:
the Eagle toppled not by war
but Bank flu, chemleaks, or partisan pit bulls'
infected bites.

Our digital twitches accrete in secret vaults,
our momentary whims and cravings
heaped like guano, mined for fuel.
They give us our receipts; their copy
is our Dorian Gray, secreted in their attics,
all our wrinkles, scars, peccadillos saved,
saved, saved.

The Stepford-dream clawed open, breath-thin veneer
is stripped and tangled. Layered wires beneath
all lead to Rome, to Caesar's ears.
He hires the largest, keenest ones—top-priced.
He longs to erase them as he does emails
when done. But these bipedal foreigners,
god-particles in our system, take their memories home.
There are no mental chastity belts.

The Wiretappers' Ball is held—location undisclosed;
reporters banned (public burned)—to brag
and swap techniques. The cars pull up
outside the hall; the charcoal silk suits
hide iPoded ears, broadband cigarette cases.
No one goes in who's not "packing."

The trophy wives glitter
like trained parakeets, but mute. Erase that—
these men go in alone. For their ears only.
The ballroom cleared of bugs by master-sweeps—
each has his portable disrupter, just in case.

Forget Joe Six-Pack! Joe Wiretap's our guy—
if information's our new currency, he tops Bill Gates.
Big Brother's now a termite colony:
voracious, ferocious—a team can strip the flesh
from any fool who falls asleep on their hill.
Rip Van Public wakes a skeleton.

We are cabbage for their shredders—
flayed, our parings kept for voodoo jabs.
Their acid topicality has stripped our spinal sheath,
set us Vitus dancing, helpless knee-jerks
they dodge as swift as shadows.
Our investigations are flypaper for dragons.

They know who we are; oh, yes—
they know who we are.

When Joe Blows

Wherever pressure is applied
there is uncertainty—a thick steel wall
can buckle, blast, blow.
Afterwards they blame weak welds.

The screws applied and tightened;
the pressure builds each day.
What one of us sits easy? Layoffs, illness,
family feuds, foreclosures—see the steam rise.

Decades of dancing on razors, skating
on cracking ice; our muscles groan.
The scream rises, is choked back.
But who has checked each and every weld?

The "mad as hell" are letting loose—
a brain blast melts their off switch
and their madness shrapnels
the neighborhood with real lead.

Interlude

The Love Song of G. Dubya Bushwack

with deep homage to T. S. Eliot

Let us go then, USA,
While the nation's fed up against this guy
And like a patient etherized on CNN cable;
Let us go, through Baghdad's half-deserted streets,
Their muddling retreats
And restless blight of greedy oil cartels
And vapor masks and mortar shells:
Ambassadors follow with a tedious argument
Of insidious intent
To lead you to an overwhelming question...

Oh, do not ask, "What is it?"
Let us pay Iraq a visit.

In the room Dick Cheney comes and goes
Plotting Saddam Hussein's overthrow.

The pettifog who silks his back with undeserving gains,
The callow dog who's spying at your window panes,
Sticked his nose into the corners of all your believings,
Lingered by the fools who chat on trains,
Let fall upon his back the chump who falls for brokerage
Schemes in the office, made a sudden leap,
And seeing that he'd informed on all his friends to Ridge,
Curled back under his rock and fell asleep.

And indeed there will be time
For the callow dog who slides along the street,
Grubbing for tattletales through your window panes;
There will be time, there will be time
To prepare a face to fool the faces that we beat;
There will be time to murder and create
Excuses for all the works of covert hands

That lift and drop the onus on our plate:
Time to press the U.N., and time for me
To steamroll past a hundred indecisions,
Ignore a hundred visions and revisions,
Before the taking of Ar-Ramadi.

In the room Dick Cheney comes and goes
Plotting Saddam Hussein's overthrow.

    And indeed there will be time
To wonder, "Do I dare?" and "Do I dare?"—
Time to turn back and consult with Blair,
With Ariel Sharon still in my hair—
(They will say, "How his reasoning's growing thin!")
My flack, dear Fletcher, will take it firmly on the chin,
And Rumsfeld, rich and modest, but asserting that we'll win—
(They will say: "But what happened to ol' Bin?")
Do I dare
Disturb the universe?
In a minute there is time
For decisions and revisions which a Minuteman will reverse.

    For I have known the real players, known them all:
Have wooed them evenings, mornings, afternoons,
I have measured out truth with coffee spoons;
I know how to win the whole Congressional
Gang with the profits from an oil boom.
        So how should I presume?

    And I have known the liberals already, known them all—
The critics fix you in a formulated phrase,
And when I am formulated, sprawling on a pin,
When I am pinned and wriggling on the wall,
Then how should I begin
To spin out my version of my crazy ways?
        And how should I presume?

And I have bought the arms already, bought them all—
Arms that are massive, launching in midair
(That made my cronies billionaires!)
    Is it Hussein's sheer excess
    That makes me so digress?
Arms that seek out depots, or on civilians fall.
    So should I then presume?
        And how should I begin?

· · · · · ·

    Shall I say, I have sent my spies through narrow streets...
They watched the smoke that rises from the plants
Of devious mobile fact'ries leaving Baghdad in fleets? ...

I should have made a loophole clause for
Scuttling Resolution 1441 with ease.

· · · · · ·

    And meanwhile North Korea sleeps so peacefully!
Smoothed by grift bringers,
Asleep...expired...or it malingers,
Stretched toward nuclear mischief, here beside you and me.
Should I, after Chirac criticizes,
Have the strength to force the moment to its crisis?
But though I have fumed and blasted, frowned and brayed,
Though I have seen my head (through digital prowess) brought
        in upon a platter,
I reap the profit—and they're no great matter;
I have seen the moment of my greatness flicker,
And I have seen the electoral Footman hold my coat, and
        snicker,
    But being rich, was not afraid.

    And would it have been worth it, after all,
After the briefings, the leaks, the planned duplicity,
Among the Congress, the talk of Homeland Security,
Would it have been worth while,
To have bitten off the matter with a smile,
To have squeezed my rationale into a ball

To roll it towards Dems' overwhelming questions,
To say: "Here is Halliburton, come from the dead,
Come back to tell you all, they shall tell you all"—
If one, handing me a billion as a figurehead
    Should say: "That is not what I meant at all;
        That is not it, at all."

    And would it have been worth it, after all,
Would it have been worth while,
After the protests and the emails and the orange alerts,
After the polls, after the court challenges, after the stock prices
        that trail along the floor—
And this, and so much more?—
It is impossible that they say just what they mean!
But as if a media spindoc turned the opposition to applause on a
        TV screen:
Would it have been worth while
If one, settling a lawsuit or shaving off a decimal,
And turning toward the window, should say: "That is not
        it at all,
    That is not what I meant, at all."

                    . . . . . .

    No! I am not Lincoln, nor was meant to be;
Am a covert planner, one that will do
To swell a progress, start a scene or two,
Advise the GOP; no doubt, an easy tool,
Deferential, glad to be of use,
Politic, cautious, and meticulous;
Full of high sentence, but a bit obtuse;
At times, indeed, almost ridiculous—
Almost, at times, the Fool.

I grow old...I grow old...
I shall watch the consequences of the war unfold.

    Shall I leave my notes behind? Do I dare to get impeached?
I shall privatize the gov'ment, and leave the budget beached.

I have heard the Four Horsemen singing, each to each.
I do not think that they will sing to me.

I have seen them riding seaward on the waves
Combing the white hair of the waves blown back
When nuclear wind blows the water white and black.

We have malingered by the piles of war debris
By seagulls wreathed with oily seaweed dead and brown,
Till Apocalyptic voices wake us, and we drown.

· · · · · ·

— IV —

Paradoxy

The oceans burn, and all along the shore,
seabirds scream a dirge and dance;
their footsteps cuneiform the myth
that we're unfolding: greasy, black, indelible;
an ulcerous tale that drills itself through veins
and whines in sleepless ears.

We've conquered Night and lost the stars—
our legions dream prescripted anthrax fears
and feast on pesticidal soup. There's warning signs
on mother's milk, and what we spurn we
ship to trusting countries lacking legal sharks.
I'll sue, I'll sue, and bankrupt you.
American refrain.

All Hail the Kingdom of McDream
where love and all its variations carry
trademarks and the franchise rights!
Our bodies teem with logos; our streets
with signs like gadflies plague our sight.
Incessant tunes drill slogans in our heads. We're
not consumers but consumptives,
poisoned by extruded needs, sucking Circe's teat.
What pigs.

What's the slogan of *your* life?
Gotta have a slogan: something easy,
something free (or they won't count you);
free of meaning, free of blame—
get it trademarked, register your DNA
or they will do it first and reap the premiums of your life.

All Hail the Fiefdom of McDream where
Armageddon parties crowd Israeli Friday nights
and bookstores list the Dummy's Guide

to Nuclear Collapse (duct tape and plastic).
Oh, dream me up a thousand nights of tales
to lull the masses: how big-spurred men so bravely
stole the reins from frankly puzzled partisans
and over-rode supreme.

In Emerald City, all must wear eyeglasses
tinted green. Vote carefully; you'll want
someone to blame. (And those who think that they
have shelter do not understand the nature of the storm.)
We watch with moral rigor mortis as Somalis
starve on primetime (*Hey, is this Survivor?*
Dude, how young they look!)
and couples parlay marriage-baiting
into millions. While we look on.

The specters of a thousand histories
cry unheard and fade in laser's glare.
Almighty Now has swept all archetypes
beneath the steal-slick surface
built to frame our thoughts, while D.C.
brews a jabberwock of reasons
for impending war, their weaponry of
mass presumption ranged to blast
opposing views to ash(croft). Wouldst thou protest?
Your soundbite's like a flea
in Titan's ear. Get thee to a gunnery.

Web

Ah, brave New World! they cried
back when ARPAnet was text-only, and "live"
meant lines scrolling up a green screen
as fast as the group could type—rumors
of pictures still impossibly wild.

As the screens shrink toward Dick Tracy watches
and magic glasses place genies on your eyes,
the corralled factoids are moored in server farms
in Podunk towns lacking other potential.

Your windows are magical with polychromed news,
any questions answered a million ways—and which is true?
All sense of fragility, of blackout,
fade behind the scintillating parade.

Awash in a sea of knowledge,
little islands of fulfilled desires,
we drift further apart. The strands that link us
leave us oddly stranded.

Voices

You ask me if I hear voices. Yes.
They drill my mind like ants
build caves in sand.

I hear the reedy whine of children playing
at the daycare up the hill. Insurance
salesmen collar me at red lights,

from other cars. I hear
Elvis shout down Baez as I
stroll from shop to shop, and

ever in the spaces of my brain the thrums
of endless rock and roll songs beat
me senseless with their verse.

We are full of voices, transmitters
humming culture's hypnotic
cues and cries.

Hear voices? How can I not?
Lately I've begun to envy
Beethoven's brave, deaf ears.

Disposable

Somewhere in that hospital file,
behind the lab reports and charts,
is the teen whose youth
was passed like bad news
down a gauntlet of kin,
who knows that solemn faces
will condemn him to blank walls
and voiceless days—
a child whose heart broke
long before his voice, whose
hope hangs shredded
like his jeans.

Can you find the page?
A palimpsest beneath the five-point list
of all his twists and flaws,
a brief description of the soul he was
and might have been.

This one small fruit, plucked and tossed,
is one of thousands—
the stinking piles mount,
as America leaves its young
on the golden altars of greed.

Disposable like so much else,
he knows he'll be tossed—
when hasn't he been tossed?
What chance his small life
in the mandibles
of flash culture?

Our do-good machines
are oiled by the pulped lives
of our victims.

The Doors Are Closing

As the streetcar pauses, docking
by Twelfth Street downtown

    the doors open to your left

the sleek white car is dotted
by a few riders caught
in travel's somnambulism,
staring with blank eyes.

On the platform, a young man—
dark hair an anti-halo,
deep coal eyes, black cloth jacket,
jeans; a dark star,
a life imploding that tugs invisibly.
He watches those exiting
as they bend to the wind,
an open-mouth gape that begs,
but he does not ask.

    the doors are closing

He lopes down the street
of twinkle-lighted trees, red-green wreaths;
stops by a jeweler's, glances up
at gold frames-in-frames—
a window with gems on black velvet.

Wind whips his coat,
his hair an ebony pearl
against white marble—
looking up
as a tailored couple inside
huddles over some trinket,

his gaze a black hole
that they miss
in their golden absorption.

the doors are closing

The train slides out of the station
swallowed by night. Head lowered,
he moves on, against the wind.

Thrift Store Christmas

There is always a trace of mold,
a stale *melange au trailer court*;
always a faint sense I'm disturbing
some great-aunt *dishabille* at home.

Even the holidays, with a surge
of red geegaws and fake greens,
don't exactly lift the mood.
This is not *It's a Wonderful Life*
unless it's Pottersville.

The crammed cases, castoffs
from shuttered stores, hold chipped gifts
chaotic on chipped shelves.
A gaggle of pot lids huddle by a clutch of glasses
emblazoned with fossilized sayings.

Aisles are by default; plenty of dead ends
and no one here has heard of "accessibility."
Labels on collapsing corrugated file drawers
as outdated as a 1980s *TV Guide*
or those Atkins diet books stacked under
the dog-eared picture Bibles.

The clerks seem a bit chipped, too—
gleaned from a workforce
already skimmed by McDonald's
and the recycling plant. The bottle-redhead smiles;
the stubbled elder too grim, salvaging a day
that might otherwise be blurred. Some are challenged
by the task of reading tags, totting up dimes—
rarely up to five bucks—
some tap keys while engrossed in family
feud by phone. I note their story lines, discard them
as implausible.

At the door, in red marker:
Free toy with each purchase.
I take home a sad-eyed beagle
in a red Santa hat.

Curing Cassandra

This won't hurt, they promise,
but the bolts from Zeus
that pierce her skull are hot agony.
Crying out, gagged by some wooden bar,
she can't even remember
why she let them do this.
Just two more, they say
and call forth lightning again
and again. *Oh gods!*
Pain tears through her head
and shudders down her limbs;
she jolts and twitches
against the hard couch.
The world has gone soft
or she has.

*There now, that wasn't bad
was it?* some face asks, wavering
in front of her renegade eyes.
Who is asking? Why?
Soft face—a woman's, smiling—
she can't put anything
in context, not even the man
standing calmly to the side, saying,
*Now you won't be bothered
by all those bad dreams.*

Siri

tells each of you
a different answer.

This copter overhead is not a drone.
But it could be.

The beep of a truck reversing
sounds like a cardiac monitor.

In blue sky unetched by contrails,
turkey vultures flap and soar,

admitting nothing.

Our pixilated lives wait
to vanish in a silent burst,

when the invisible power we pulse with
suddenly

ends.

Remove All Cookies

Sly footsteps following yours.
Blips betraying your innermost boredom.
Beacon, action tag, nano-snitch
selling your secrets cheap. You don't even get royalties.

Cell phones whisper to store cameras—
they have you typed, targeted, tamed.
Little shopper, little worker bee—
your digital pheromones are spread out promiscuously,
indicting your days—and nights—
irreversible datatattooes.

Your DNA's swiped at the lab—
some guy's constructing faces from trash—
your license and credit card scanned and traveling the world
without you. Romanian home business,
cloning your ID. Mosquito drones
eye your backyard sunbathing, 90 images/second.
Waiting only for celebrity to hit.

How can we *not* pray for someone
to trip over the power cord, tsunami-surge
the secreted stuff, and plunge the world
into sweet ignorance again?

The Day I Nuked the Romans

The tension had been building:
They surrounded my best cities,
stepping over the border every chance
they got, then a step back,
apologetic façade, and they'd start
tormenting again.

But I had never used
the Ultimate Weapon; never
let the million-pixeled simulacrum descend
in any of the hundred wars waged
through the many flat-screened ages,
through the nights of staring at flailing
soldiers the size of large ants;
nights I ignored my poetry, my dishes,
conquering the worlds I didn't live in,
avoiding the one I did.

Fear of some karma held me,
a little voice whispering that it *did* matter;
the tiny nuke was my intent
and Rubicons could be as small as thought.

That night I turned away
from the whisper, joined the thousands
(*millions*?) who called it a game,
who killed, raped, stole in full-color fantasies,
whose fingers pushed the button
again and again.

And it did become easier; the next night
Paris fell, and Poona—any city I could reach
to pummel my enemies. For, after all,
what harm could a computer game
do?

Pyongyang

is trembling
like a cocked gun—hearts thrumming,
hunger thrust aloft on a three-part spear.

Houseflies crawl over the lips
of gaunt, listless babies—
winged intruders gesturing like Pilate.
They pose like aircraft, wings glinting, for flight.

Okinawa's rockets bracket the sky,
fueled and hefty, aerodynamically eager
to meet intruders.

From space, US ships look like flies
on the ocean's cobalt. Half the world
is tinderbox.

Half is a match.

Startled, *Drosophila* scramble and zoom,
madly evading capture—then settle back
everywhere, to feed on death

and sweet decay.

Channel Surfing: High Tide

"We interrupt to bring you urgent news...."
Hon, change the channel; see what else is on.
Sick of hearing panic over flu—

the daily counts, school closures—you refuse
to think about it—urgency long gone
despite interruptions with emergent news.

Pandemic? What pandemic? That's for losers.
I'm fit and healthy; and kids belong
in schools—not hearing panic over flu!

Unconcerned with CDC's and WHO's
world plans, or if we've crossed a Rubicon,
when they interrupt with urgent news

you turn away, confidently snooze.
Prepping's just not in your lexicon;
you're sick of hearing panic over flu!

Happy ostrich, live your life, obtuse;
watch *Lost* and *Idol* till your chance is gone.
They interrupt to bring you urgent news,
but you're too sick—and feeling panic over flu.

Avatar

While downtown bleeds off
another few stores, and acid rain carves
red brick into glacial moraine—
garbage piling like erratics

on the city floor—show me vast
purple landscapes, pixel-perfect
plains; I want to touch them,
let them flow over me, 3-D.

Show me myself in blue-green skin,
cornrows dangling like whips;
show the world's destruction, but
let me hope. Let me dream.

Feed me the hero, so much braver than I
yet down to earth—a pal, with inner grit
(like mine, I'm sure), atomic courage
blowing apart all snares and cunning.

Let me sit in gently rocking cushioned seats
with a ton of buttered popcorn, a quart of pop,
my "real life" glowing, wall-sized before me.
Race, fight, love, win—moving nothing more
than hand to mouth.

Not a Gambler

There's never the lust for chance
nor guiltless pocketing of windfalls,
no scooping of heaps the others lose.
I long for the *cert*, the sure thing,
holding tight to the little I have.
How, then, do I live
in this dicey world,
in these blossom-snapping, drought-and-deluge,
heart-ripping, three-card-monte moments
when nothing—oh, *nothing*—is guaranteed?
Not even taxes. Maybe death.
But even that is a daily six-sided throw.
The cross-beaked rooster dances
his mating steps—he's a week away from the stewpot—
does he care? Even *I* am Fate,
same as the inky cloud that fingers the sun,
the tiny hole in my tire that blows
in one crazy swerving minute, the hollow oak
that finally lets go. The rooster dances
atop his hen. Roll...and roll again.

Escape

Slowly, like a princess enmeshed in thorns,
she recognized peril and withdrew.
She loosed her fingers from networked keystrokes,
wandered away from news that watched her too,
saved her opinions for voice and paper.

The clever jangle of ringtones ceased;
four-color tsunamis receded;
the world stopped telling her she was important
and a valued customer. She stopped carrying
plastic numbers that revealed her position
on everything.

Eventually, the world grew smaller,
slowed, and leafed out before her cleared gaze.
She was only where she was; she had
what she could see and touch
and what was shimmering inside.
And, once again, the arc of the sun
was an uninterrupted miracle.

Acknowledgments

Grateful acknowledgment is made to the editors of the following publications and presses for first publishing these poems or earlier versions of them:

Bird's Eye Review: "Suburb on the Edge of Nowhere"
Blast Furnace: "False Equivalence"
Bolts of Silk: "Japan Washes Ashore in Oregon"
Centrifugal Eye: "Eating at the Poorhouse"
Denali: "Saturday: Anytown"
Diverse Voices: "Demeter Moment"
Elohi Gadusi Journal: "Can You Outrun a Tsunami," "Symbiosis"
Flutter: "Thrift Store Christmas"
Foghorn: "Kubla Can't"
FutureCycle Poetry: "For the 21st Century: Elegy on Six Monitors"
Green Fuse: "Squatter's Flag"
Melusine: "Curing Cassandra"
Mreview: "Paradoxy," "Shadows," "Disposable" (as "Tossed Life")
New Verse News: "Avatar," "The Apocalypse Goes Unnoticed
    in Newtown, CT," "Cleveland: Unlucky Number," "Gary,"
    "Living On Food Stamps and the $150 They Get From Nielsen,"
    "Pit Stop," "Six-Course Apocalypse"
Northville Review: "The Day I Nuked the Romans"
Out Of Line: "Non-Zen-sical" (as "I'm Praying for the Zen View")
Pacific Review: "Foreclosure"
Pilgrimage: "Remove All Cookies"
Poets Against the War: "[The] Love Song of G. Dubya Bushwack"
Portland Lights: "Drought in the Garden"
Post Poetry: "Synchronicities," "Wiretapper's Ball"
River Poets Journal: "Ticking Over the New Year"
Rougarou: "Grand Street North"
Tenpenny Players: "Century Farm"
The Quizzical Chair: "The Doors are Closing"
the storm is coming: "When Joe Blows"
Untitled Country: "Salmonelle" (as "Afterimage")

"Demeter Moment" and "Curing Cassandra" appeared in the chapbook *Palimpsests* (Uttered Chaos, 2011).

Thank you to Rhetorical Devices, Poetic License, and all my poet friends in Oregon for their support, insight and critique. Thanks to my dear friends and my family for their encouragement. And thanks to Diane Kistner and the FutureCycle Press team for their hard work and patience with me.

Cover artwork, "Chernobyl Amusement Park Karts (Pripyat, northern Ukraine)" by Shanomag.com, third-place winner of the Mother Nature Strikes Back Photo Challenge (May 2015); cover and interior book design by Diane Kistner; Avenir text and titling

About FutureCycle Press

FutureCycle Press is dedicated to publishing lasting English-language poetry books, chapbooks, and anthologies in both print-on-demand and Kindle ebook formats. Founded in 2007 by long-time independent editor/publishers and partners Diane Kistner and Robert S. King, the press incorporated as a nonprofit in 2012. A number of our editors are distinguished poets and writers in their own right, and we have been actively involved in the small press movement going back to the early seventies.

The FutureCycle Poetry Book Prize and honorarium is awarded annually for the best full-length volume of poetry we publish in a calendar year. Introduced in 2013, our Good Works projects are anthologies devoted to issues of universal significance, with all proceeds donated to a related worthy cause. Our Selected Poems series highlights contemporary poets with a substantial body of work to their credit; with this series we strive to resurrect work that has had limited distribution and is now out of print.

We are dedicated to giving all of the authors we publish the care their work deserves, making our catalog of titles the most diverse and distinguished it can be, and paying forward any earnings to fund more great books.

We've learned a few things about independent publishing over the years. We've also evolved a unique, resilient publishing model that allows us to focus mainly on vetting and preserving for posterity poetry collections of exceptional quality without becoming overwhelmed with bookkeeping and mailing, fundraising activities, or taxing editorial and production "bubbles." To learn more about what we do, come see us at www.futurecycle.org.

The FutureCycle Poetry Book Prize

All full-length volumes of poetry published by FutureCycle Press in a given calendar year are considered for the annual FutureCycle Poetry Book Prize. This allows us to consider each submission on its own merits, outside of the context of a contest. Too, the judges see the finished book, which will have benefitted from the beautiful book design and strong editorial gloss we are famous for.

The book ranked the best in judging is announced as the prize-winner in the subsequent year. There is no fixed monetary award; instead, the winning poet receives an honorarium of 20% of the total net royalties from all poetry books and chapbooks the press sold online in the year the winning book was published. The winner is also accorded the honor of being on the panel of judges for the next year's competition; all judges receive copies of all contending books to keep for their personal library.

www.ingramcontent.com/pod-product-compliance
Lightning Source LLC
Chambersburg PA
CBHW072358090426
42741CB00012B/3077

* 9 7 8 1 9 4 2 3 7 1 1 5 1 *